Jersey
A Third Selection
IN OLD PHOTOGRAPHS

Jersey
A Third Selection

IN OLD PHOTOGRAPHS

Collected by RAOUL LEMPRIERE

Alan Sutton Publishing Limited
Phoenix Mill · Far Thrupp
Stroud · Gloucestershire

First published in 1993

British Library Cataloguing in Publication Data

Lemprière, Raoul
  Jersey in Old Photographs: Third Selection
  I. Title
  942.341

ISBN 0-7509-0369-4

Typeset in 9/10 Sabon.
Typesetting and origination by
Alan Sutton Publishing Limited.
Printed in Great Britain by
Redwood Books, Trowbridge.

Contents

Introduction

Interest in old photographs has greatly increased during recent years, and instead of their being thoughtlessly thrown away many are now preserved and reproduced in books, magazines and newspapers, recalling for those who see them memories of times gone by. The photographs in this book are derived from a number of sources, including my own collection of photographs, postcards and books made over some forty-five years, and span the period from the 1870s to the 1970s.

In order to appreciate and fully understand the photographs it is necessary to know a little about Jersey and its way of life during the period represented.

Jersey has an area of 45 square miles and is the largest of the Channel Islands, the most southerly of the British Isles. At the closest point it is about 15 miles from the west coast of Normandy. Jersey is a bailiwick comprising the main island and a number of islets, notably the Ecréhous and the Minquiers. The population at the beginning of the period covered by this book was 56,627 (1871) and by the end had increased to 72,629 (1971). The island is divided into twelve ancient parishes, each of which is an administrative district presided over by a constable (mayor). The capital is the town of Saint Helier which lies approximately halfway along the south coast. It occupies a large part of the parish of the same name and overspills into neighbouring parishes.

Since 1066, except for a few short breaks, the most recent of which was the German occupation (1940–45), Jersey has been part of the English (later British) Dominions. The Sovereign is represented in the island by a lieutenant-governor. The Chief Magistrate and President of the States Assembly (the legislature) is the Bailiff, before whom in the Royal Court, in the States, and on special occasions is carried a magnificent silver-gilt mace. This was presented to Jersey by King Charles II as proof of his royal affection towards the island in which he had been twice received in safety during the Civil War, when he was excluded from the remainder of his realm.

The photographs are divided into seven sections dealing respectively with the Town of Saint Helier and its Suburbs, Coast and Country, Agriculture, Summertime, The Battle of Flowers, Royal Connections, and People and Events.

Saint Helier, like most other towns during the early part of the period covered, had many small, privately owned shops, the proprietors of which more often than not 'lived over the shop'. 'The town', as it was commonly called, was the hub of the island, with the seat of government, the Royal Court House, the markets, the principal shops, the leading hotels, numerous public houses and the main harbour. It was quite large and had increased greatly in size since the beginning of the nineteenth century. Since the Liberation in 1945 the town has undergone great changes and many of the privately owned shops have disappeared, along with much else.

Jersey's coast and country were wholly unspoilt until after the First World War, when a certain amount of undesirable development took place. There were the twelve ancient parish churches, water-mills and windmills, beautiful granite farmhouses, a number of fine mansions, old cottages, many of them thatched, hotels and public houses, and many fortifications dating from the thirteenth to the nineteenth century. Since the Liberation a great deal of the countryside has been lost to development, but fortunately much remains unspoilt.

The principal industry was agriculture until some years after the Liberation, particularly the growing and exporting of 'Jersey Royal' potatoes and tomatoes, and, to a lesser extent, the rearing and exporting of the beautiful Jersey cattle, still the only breed allowed on the island. Tourism was also very important. Since the Liberation this has gradually changed, until now when the finance industry has become all-important with tourism in second place and agriculture in decline.

In addition to a network of roads and lanes, the island had from the early 1870s two railways, one that ran from Saint Helier to Saint Aubin, continued to Corbière in 1899, and the other from Saint Helier to Gorey (Gorey Village), ultimately extended to Gorey Pier in 1891. The former was closed in 1936 and the latter in 1929. Communication with the outside world was solely by sea, mainly through the port of Saint Helier, until the advent of a regular air service in the 1930s.

Down the centuries Britain maintained a garrison in Jersey and continued to do so until 1926. In addition there was the Royal Militia, one of the most ancient forces of the Crown, of which the island was immensely proud. It remained in being until the Second World War but was not revived after the Liberation.

Ever since peace descended on Europe in 1815 Jersey has been visited each year by ever increasing numbers of visitors, and by the end of the century it was to have a substantial tourist industry which continued growing well into the twentieth century. This accounted for the large number of hotels and guest houses in the island, the excursion cars and char-à-bancs with their guides, the summer shows in the Triangle Park and Springfield Grounds, and much else besides.

Up to the Second World War farmers and country people were principally of old Jersey stock and still for the most part spoke Jersey Norman-French as well as English. In the town of Saint Helier were to be found, in addition to the local people, many families, mostly from the United Kingdom, some of whom had been established only for a generation or two or who had recently settled there. There were also a number of French families who had taken up residence since

1815. In addition there was a considerable non-native resident population, consisting largely of retired naval and army officers who, with the principal native families and the officers of the garrison, formed their own social circles. Since the Liberation the proportion of native islanders in the total population has been much reduced.

'Events' here were much as elsewhere, although the Battle of Flowers dating from 1902 and a few other occasions could claim to be local.

The period before the Second World War was one of stability and gradual change. The framework of life was well established. The family was the unit in which people lived. There was discipline in the home, at school, at work and in honorary service, whether in the States, in the parishes or in the Royal Militia. Church-going and attendance at Sunday School were the rule rather than the exception. Despite a hard lifestyle, with none of the present-day labour-saving devices, and a certain amount of poverty, many were able to gain a great deal of enjoyment and satisfaction out of life. Since the Liberation all of that has changed, and the island has followed the same trends as elsewhere in the British Isles.

Throughout the period there were always a number of well-established photographers in Jersey such as Asplet & Green, E. Baudoux, P. Godfray, A. Laurens, C.P. Ouless, Albert Smith, E. Hamilton Toovey and Tynan Bros., to mention but a few. In addition there were the postcard and other professional photographers from outside the island, and numerous amateurs. The work of professional, postcard and amateur photographers is represented here.

I would like to take this opportunity to thank the following for lending me photographs for reproduction in this book: A. Amy & Son Ltd, Ann Street Brewery Co. Ltd, Mrs B.I. Breton, Browne's Fashion House, Cooper & Co., Mrs L.S. Copp, Mr R.S. Cox, Mr Roy Heaven, *Jersey Evening Post*, Jersey Motor Transport Co. Ltd, Mr P.W. Loftus, Mr I.R. Monins, Mrs H.I.D. Muir, Mrs Q. Quénault, Mr K. C. Renault, Mr L.E. Samson, Springfield Entertainments Ltd, Mrs D.G. Taylor, Mr H.J. Vibert and Voisin & Co. I would also like to thank Mr Cox for help so readily given, the Jersey Library Reference Department, the States of Jersey Postal Administration and Fort Regent Leisure Centre for their kind assistance, Mr R. Briault for preparing the photographs for publication, and Mrs V. Butlin and Miss A. Shalamon for typing the introduction and captions.

Raoul Lemprière
Jersey, May 1993

SECTION ONE

The Town of Saint Helier and its Suburbs

Staff group, Ann Street Brewery Co. Ltd, Ann Street. The brewery was almost certainly established by J.S. Palmer, probably in 1871. (*c.* 1900)

Staff outing, Ann Street Brewery Co. Ltd. The group is outside the Great Eastern Hotel, St John. For an uninterrupted view of the front of the hotel see *A Second Selection*, p. 73. (*c.* 1900)

W. White, family baker, confectioner & grocer, 39 Bath Street. (In or before 1895)

W. White, 39 Bath Street, the tea room. (In or before 1895)

J.G. Quénault, Ironmonger & Jersey Milk Can Factory, 32 Bath Street. Note the Jersey milk cans above the fascia of the shop and in the left of the window. (*c.* 1909)

J.T. Bigwood, stationer and printer, 45
Bath Street. (Early this century)

Soleil Levant, café and restaurant, Bath Street. French agricultural workers are gathered
outside. (Early this century)

Wests Cinema, on the corner of Bath Street and Peter Street. It was opened in 1923 and closed in 1972. (1956)

Tommy Arnold and his band, Plaza Ballroom, Bath Street. (1939)

Dancing in progress at the Plaza Ballroom. (1939)

Victoria Club (by A. Curry, 1894), Beresford Street. (In or before 1898)

Orviss Limited (established 1874), on the corner of Beresford Street and Halkett Street. (*c.* 1934)

The grocery department of Orviss Ltd, where customers would place their orders while comfortably seated on the chairs provided. (*c.* 1934)

The bacon counter (right), Orviss Ltd, where bacon was sliced to the customer's requirements. (*c.* 1934)

Orviss Ltd, Beresford House, Beresford Street, almost opposite the main shop. (*c.* 1934)

The confectionery department, Orviss Ltd, Beresford House. (*c.* 1934)

The hardware department, Orviss Ltd, Beresford House. (*c.* 1934)

The charcuterie, Orviss Ltd, 22a Beresford Street. (*c.* 1934)

The greengrocery department, Orviss Ltd, 22 Beresford Street. (*c.* 1934)

Orviss Ltd, travellers' cars and delivery vans drawn up on Victoria Avenue, beside the Lower Park. In the background, to the right, is West Park Pavilion, now enlarged and called the Inn on the Park. (c. 1934)

Mr John W. Orviss who founded Orviss Ltd in 1874.

Orviss Ltd staff outing at Rozel Bay Hotel, St Martin. For photographs of the exterior and interior of the hotel see *A Second Selection*, p. 75. (Early this century)

Frs. J. GRANDIN & Co.,

Iron Founders and Merchants,
Furnishing Ironmongers, &c.,

13 and 15, BURRARD STREET, and

27, COMMERCIAL BUILDINGS, JERSEY.

Our Jersey Ranges

Are noted for Economy in Working, and consequent satisfaction in use.

A large variety of Heating and Cooking Stoves.

THE NEW FAVOURITE FRENCH PATTERN RANGES.
SMITH & WESTWOOD'S CELEBRATED STOVES.

DOULTON WARE STOVES AND KERBS.
HEARTH TILES, FENDERS, &c.

MARBLE AND ENAMELLED SLATE CHIMNEY PIECES.
GAS TUBES AND FITTINGS.

REPAIRS TO ENGINES, MACHINERY, BOILERS, &c.

Frs. J. Grandin & Co. advertisement with illustration of a 'Jersey Range.' (1898)

Jupe's (A.E. Jupe), grocers, 18 Burrard Street (north side), on the corner of Halkett Place (west side). (In or before 1913)

Irish Yard, Cannon Street. The property no doubt acquired its name because many of the original occupiers came from Ireland. It was demolished and replaced by flats and is now known as Parade Square. (1963)

Irish Yard, Cannon Street. (1963)

Roof-top view of the markets bordering Cattle Street and Minden Place. Grove Place chapel is in the distance (centre) with the spire of St Mark's church to the right. (Late nineteenth century)

Market (probably the fish market) bordering Cattle Street. (Late nineteenth century)

W. White's A.B.C. Tea Rooms, Cattle Street. Note the Jersey simnels in the bottom left of the right window and the bottom right of the left window. (In or before 1898)

Church House, Church Street, St Helier. This was demolished and replaced by Norwich Union House. (1968)

G.E. Croad, funeral directors, 35 & 37 Colomberie. This building has since been demolished.

No. 48 Colomberie. The Victorian shop front was removed to the Jersey Museum in 1958. (In or shortly before 1958)

Nos 7, 9 and 11 Conway Street (east side). These buildings have since been demolished. (Late 1950s or early '60s)

Bartlett's Victoria Hotel, on the corner of Conway Street (west side) and Esplanade. To the right of centre is the Westaway Memorial. For another photograph of the memorial see *Jersey in Old Photographs*, p. 58. (Between 1875 and 1888)

Penfold Pillar Box, outside Drivehire, 26 David Place, at one time the premises of Down Bros. Excelsior Stables. The pillar box, dating from between 1866 and 1879, was removed from David Place. It is one of two belonging to the States, one of which is in the Central Market and the other in the piazza at Fort Regent. (1950s or '60s)

The Methodist church, Royal Crescent, Don Road. This church once stood at the centre of the crescent. It has since been demolished and the site left vacant. This photograph was taken from the site where Berkeley Court now stands. (1950s or '60s)

Nos 37 and 39 Don Street (now known as Westaway Chambers). Protruding from the façade is a stone bearing the initials N.W. and A.A. and the date 1811. (1964)

The garden frontage of F.C.J. (Convent School), David Place. The building was demolished and replaced by blocks of flats known as Convent Court. (In or before 1969)

The Val Plaisant frontage of F.C.J. (In or before 1969)

The Junior Library, Dumaresq Street. This building, now demolished, housed the junior library from 1931 to 1963. (1963)

The front entrance of the Junior Library. (1963)

The main entrance of Fort Regent. (1964)

The outer walls on the west side of Fort Regent. (1964)

A scene of dereliction within the walls of Fort Regent. (1964)

The General Hospital, Gloucester Street. The pleasant garden has been replaced by a car park. (Early this century)

Grosvenor Street, looking west towards La Motte Street. (Early this century)

The Forum Cinema (by W.F. Hedges), Grenville Street. It was opened in 1935 and closed in 1981. The building was demolished in 1984 and replaced by blocks of offices. (1935)

The interior of the Forum Cinema, Grenville Street. The Compton organ is now in Queen's Hall, Fort Regent. (1935)

Property on Halkett Place forming the corner of Queen's Street and Hilgrove Street. For another view of the same building see *A Second Selection*, p. 28. (1873)

Halkett Place (west side). The first nine properties (counting from the right) have since been demolished. (1950s or '60s)

The fisheries, Orviss Ltd, Halkett Street, with a Christmas display of poultry and fish. (*c.* 1934)

Browne's Fashion House window display at 6 Halkett Street (west side) and Hilgrove Street (south side). (1924)

J.A. Samson, bellhangers, gasfitters, ironmongers, lamp dealers and plumbers, 14 and 16 Halkett Street. Note the bell sign above No. 14. (*c.* 1893)

A horse-drawn van belonging to J.A. Samson. (Early this century)

A J.A. Samson light lorry at the harbour. (*c.* 1925)

An A.P. Samson van by the Lower Park. (1930s)

A.P. Samson & Sons fleet of vehicles. (1960s)

The harbour at the south end of Commercial Buildings. (Before 1893)

Old shop at the corner of Hilary Street and La Motte Street. The building has now been demolished. (1964)

Poids du Roi (King's Weights), Hilgrove Street, on the left side of the entrance to that part of the Central Market once known as The Pork Market. (1950s or '60s)

C.G. Ferbrache, 34 Hill Street. (1950s or '60s)

C.G. Ferbrache, antique and second hand dealer, 34 Hill Street. The building has since been demolished. (1950s or '60s)

Ingouville Lane. Note the old wooden bollard and gas lamp, both of which have now been removed. (1950s or '60s)

King Street (looking east from a point slightly to the east of the Brook Street junction). On the right are J. Taylor's R.M. Stores, founded in 1891, and Tregear's Oriental Tea Rooms two doors away. For a view of the interior of the tea rooms see *A Second Selection*, p. 38. (Before 1940)

King Street (looking west from its junction with Halkett Place). (In or before 1932)

La Motte House, La Motte Street. (In or before 1913)

Voisin & Co. department store, 24, 26, 28 and 30 King Street. (1890s)

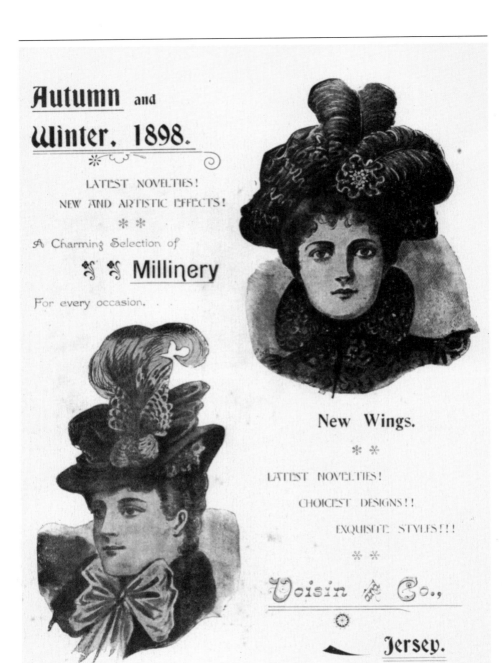

Advertisement for millinery at Voisin & Co. (1898)

Hotel du Palais de Cristal, King Street. (Early this century)

Simpson's, stationers, Library Place. The building has now been demolished. (1965)

St Columba's church (by J. Hine, 1859), Midvale Road. The spire has since been removed. (Early this century)

General view of Mulcaster Street, looking east, with Daly's Hotel (The Grapes) on the right. (Early this century)

Filleul & Queen, printers, 14 New Street. This building has been demolished and rebuilt. (1950s or '60s)

Small shop with slightly bowed window, Old Street. The shop has been demolished. (1950s or '60s)

The stage of the Alhambra, Phillips Street. The newly painted drop curtain depicts Corbiere lighthouse at its centre. (1914)

The Playhouse, New Street. This building was originally a church and latterly a hall, refronted in 1937 and converted into a theatre (architect C.W. Blanchard Bolton). From 1946 to 1963 this was the home of the Denville Players, a repertory company of which Len Laurie and Majorie Denville were the principals. (In or before 1962)

Interior of the Playhouse, New Street. (In or before 1962)

Gulliver (late Pixley), monumental masons, 34 Parade. The keystone above the arch bears the initials E P and the date 1823. (1950s or '60s)

Pier Road (east side). Much of this side of the thoroughfare has since been demolished and rebuilt. (1950s or '60s)

Pier Road (west side). Many of these buildings have also been demolished and rebuilt. (1950s or '60s)

George D. Laurens, 3 and 5 Queen Street. (Early this century)

The Little Theatre, Providence Street. The theatre was opened in 1954 and closed in 1965. It provided the island debut for such well known artistes as Shirley Bassey and Wilfred Brambell. (1956)

The Exeter, Queen Street. (Early this century)

Orviss Ltd, grocers, on the corner of Queen Street and Halkett Street. (*c.* 1934)

Old house on the west side of Roseville Street, towards the Colomberie end. The house has since been demolished. (1950s or '60s)

On the corner of Roseville Street at the junction with Colomberie. The whole block, including the corner with Green Street, has since been demolished. (1950s or '60s)

Lipscombe Ltd (established 1811), bakers and confectioners, 1 Sand Street. This shop's specialities included *Vraic* buns and Jersey wonders. (1950s or '60s)

H.J. Berry, tea stores, 6 Waterloo Street. This was the predecessor of Cooper & Company. (Early this century)

Cooper & Company van and driver. (Late 1950s or '60s)

The Star Restaurant (1948–1961), Wharf Street. This was one of the island's premier restaurants and occupied the ground floor of what had been the Star Hotel. For an earlier view of the building see *A Second Selection*, p. 51. (1950s or '60s)

Entrance to the Star Restaurant. (1950s or '60s)

Signs outside the Star Restaurant. (1950s or '60s)

Pomme d'Or Hotel and Southampton Hotel, Weighbridge, St Helier. (In or after 1899)

West Park Pavilion (sometimes referred to as 'The Tin Hut'), West Park. The building was opened on 24 May 1886 under the name of Rolland's New York Circus. (1914)

Bus belonging to Joe's Bus Service (in livery of blue and cream) parked before its journey back through town from West Park. (1946)

SECTION TWO
Coast and Country

Kiln, related sheds and stacks of bricks at Copp's Brickfields, Mont-à-l'Abbé, St Helier. The brickfields were finally operated by Mr Horace Copp. The last firing was in 1941. (In or before 1941)

A view of the base of the kiln at Copp's Brickfields. (In or before 1941)

Copp's Brickfields, giving a close view of the kiln. (In or before 1941)

Men working at Copp's Brickfields with bricks on a barrow. (In or before 1941)

A wall of stacked bricks at Copp's Brickfields. (In or before 1941)

Men at Copp's Brickfields, either at Maufant or Five Oaks, St Saviour. (Late nineteenth century or early this century)

Bellozanne Valley, St Helier. (Early this century)

Orviss Ltd, First Tower, St Helier. (*c.* 1934)

Interior of St Aubin's railway station, the scene of a grand bazaar in aid of the St Aubin's District Church Fund. (August 1871)

The Terminus Hotel, St Aubin, with a garden seat horse-drawn omnibus standing close by. (Probably Summer 1890)

Beresford Supply Stores (Orviss), St Aubin. (*c.* 1934)

St Aubin's Market, St Aubin, before its demolition. Parts of the market, notably the pillars and the poor box, were preserved and incorporated into the building that replaced it. (Late 1950s or early '60s)

The Bulwarks, St Aubin. (Mid-1870s)

Grève de Lecq, St Ouen. The Pavilion Hotel is on the left and a defensive tower is in the centre. (Late nineteenth century)

Small eighteenth-century fort, Bouley Bay, Trinity. (Late nineteenth century)

The Royal Jersey Golf Club Links, Grouville. (Late nineteenth century)

Ruined German Buildings, east side of La Rue au Blancq, St Clement. (Late 1940s or '50s)

Samarès Post Office, Inner Road, St Clement. The post office was opened in 1899 and closed in 1956. The shop remained open for some time after it had ceased to be a post office. (1950s)

Lobster pots. This interesting view shows a completed willow pot, a partially completed pot and bundles of willow. (Late 1940s or '50s)

Lookout post erected by the Germans on top of La Hougue Bie, Grouville, during the Occupation. (1940s)

The New Era Cinema, Victoria Road, St Clement. The cinema was opened in 1952 and closed in 1972.

Agriculture

A Jersey farmyard, with a haystack in the traditional shape raised on staddle stones (right foreground) and a boxcart (left background). (Early this century)

The *vraic* (seaweed) harvest. (Early this century)

A *vraic* gatherer on the beach. (In or before 1906)

Stacks of *vraic* with a view of La Rocco Tower, St Ouen's Bay, in the distance. (1962 or 1963)

Stacks of *vraic*. A similar scene looking inland. (1962 or 1963)

Digging potatoes which are being put into baskets. (Early this century)

Jersey vans loaded with potatoes, waiting near the weighbridge, St Helier. (Between 1886 and 1896)

Lorries loaded with potatoes, with their drivers, waiting on Victoria Avenue, St Helier, to be weighed at the weighbridge. (1950s)

Jersey cows grazing in a tranquil setting. (In or before 1904)

Jersey cow being milked in a meadow. (In or before 1905)

Royal Jersey Agricultural & Horticultural Society August Show at Springfield Show Grounds. (1931)

Threshing at Les Platons, Trinity. (Summer 1948)

Threshing at Les Platons, Trinity. (Summer 1948)

Haystacks being built in the traditional manner at St Martin. (Summer 1948)

SECTION FOUR

Summertime

Postcard showing a modestly dressed bathing belle supporting a lifebelt, with a view of Portelet Bay, St Brelade, inset. (In or before 1908)

The *Lydia* and the *Frederica* berthed side by side in St Helier Harbour. Both ships belonged to the London & South Western Railway Company and were completed in 1890. (Early this century)

The *Hantonia*, owned by the London & South Western Railway Company and operated out of Southampton. It became operational on the Le Havre service in 1912 and first visited the Channel Islands in 1923. (Early this century)

Saloon Lounge of the *Hantonia*. (Early this century)

The *Brittany*, owned by the Southern Railway. This ship entered service on the Jersey–St Malo route in 1933 which she operated for many years in conjunction with excursions to the other islands and some relief work. (Between 1933 and 1962)

S.S. "ISLE OF JERSEY"

The *Isle Of Jersey*, with her sister ships, the *Isle of Guernsey* and the *Isle of Sark*, was owned by the Southern Railway and operated out of Southampton for many years. She entered service in 1930. (Between 1930 and 1959)

The *Roebuck*, St Helier Harbour. This ship was owned by the Great Western Railway and entered service in 1897. (Early this century)

Aircraft on the beach at West Park, St Helier. Air travel came to the island in the 1930s. Before the opening of the airport at St Peter, aircraft landed on the beach at West Park. (In or before 1937)

Ouaisné Bay being dismantled on First Tower slipway after being damaged on landing. (August 1935)

The train from St Helier approaching First Tower railway station. (In or before 1907)

The Palace Hotel, St Saviour. This hotel was opened in 1930 and was intended to cater for the top end of the market. The building incorporated the house known as Bagatelle and had an extremely beautiful garden. A fire gutted the main part of the hotel on 7 March 1945 and it was not rebuilt. (1930s)

The dining room of the Sandringham Hotel, Colomberie, St Helier. The hotel was demolished and the site redeveloped. (Early this century)

Bouley Bay Hotel, top of Bouley Bay, Trinity. This country hotel was demolished some years ago. (Early this century)

Grouville Holiday Camp, Grouville. This catered for the cheaper end of the market. (1920s or '30s)

Group of happy holidaymakers at the Aberfeldy Hotel, Old St John's Road, St Helier. (27 June 1930)

Britannia excursion car outside the Southampton Hotel, Weighbridge. (Early this century)

Group of visitors on an A.A. Pitcher Tantivy motor char-à-banc excursion. (Early this century)

La Fosse Tea Gardens, Portelet, St Brelade. This was one of a number of tea rooms to be found throughout the island. (In or before 1907)

Bathing machines on the beach at First Tower, St Helier. (Early this century)

Paddling in the Victoria Marine Lake, West Park, St Helier. (Early this century)

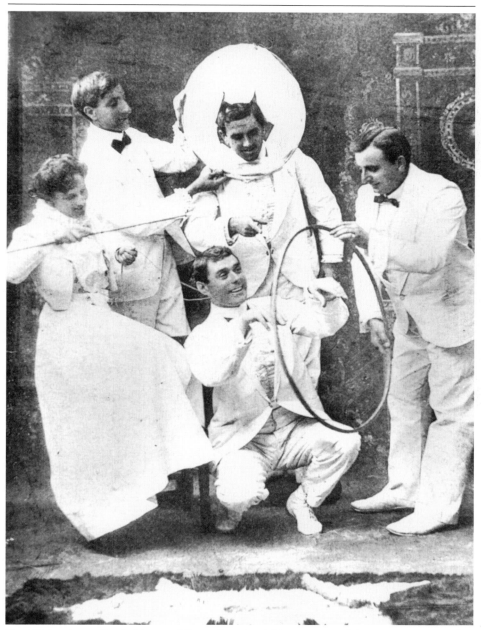

The White Coons Banjo Team while performing. This was one of the concert parties that visited Jersey during the summer and performed in the Triangle Park (now the Victoria Park) or, if wet or cold, in West Park Pavilion (now The Inn on the Park), St Helier. (Early this century)

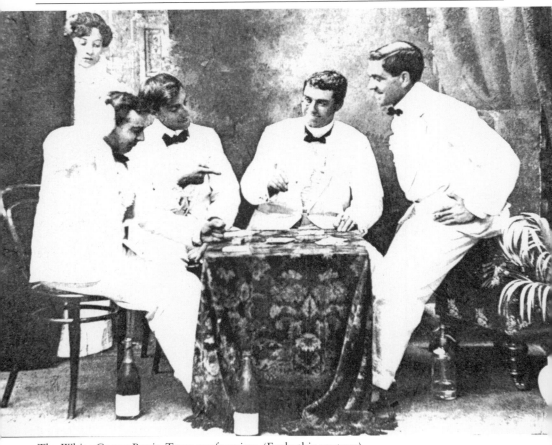

The White Coons Banjo Team performing. (Early this century)

The Battle of Flowers

The Battle of Flowers was first held on 9 July 1902 on Victoria Avenue as part of the celebrations to mark the coronation of King Edward VII and Queen Alexandra. The event proved such a success that it was held each year until and including 1913. The name 'Battle of Flowers' is derived from the fact that at one time at the end of the parade the participants and the spectators used to engage in 'battle' by pelting each other with flowers taken from the exhibits.

There was no 'Battle' in 1914 owing to the outbreak of war. The first post-war 'Battle' was held at First Tower Park on 9 August 1923. In 1928 the venue was changed to Springfield Showgrounds where it was held each year up to and including 1939. War again put a stop to the event and it was not revived until 1951 when it was held once more on Victoria Avenue, which has remained its venue ever since.

Over the years the style of the exhibits has changed considerably. Before the First World War a greater variety of flowers was used to decorate the floats and the blooms were not as closely arranged as nowadays. Between the wars the arena was filled with the scent of squashed hydrangea after the 'Battle', as that was the flower principally used to decorate the floats. Since the Second World War a wider range of flowers has been used and even paper flowers are now permitted. Most exhibits are very well designed and some of the larger ones are most spectacular.

The cover of the official programme for the Battle of Flowers, 1905.

Horse-drawn exhibit proceeding westwards along Victoria Avenue, St Helier. (In or before 1906)

General view of Victoria Avenue with a decorated motor car proceeding westwards. (In or before 1906)

Another decorated motor car proceeding along Victoria Avenue. (In or before 1907)

Four-in-hand proceeding westwards along Victoria Avenue. (1909)

Decorated horse-drawn carriage proceeding eastwards along Victoria Avenue. Boaters and sunshades are much in evidence. (1911)

Junior exhibit by the decorated entrance to the east end of Victoria Avenue, with the Grand Hotel in the background. (In or before 1912)

Decorated horse-drawn coach. (15 August 1912)

Chamber of Commerce entry, Springfield Showgrounds, St Helier. The Jersey Chamber of Commerce, founded in 1768, is reputed to be the oldest Chamber in the English-speaking world. (1935)

Coronation Coach. (Presumably 1937)

The Battle of Flowers. (Between 1928 and 1939)

The Battle of Flowers. (Between 1928 and 1939)

The Battle of Flowers. (Between 1928 and 1939)

SECTION SIX
Royal Connections

Jersey and the other Channel Islands formed part of the Duchy of Normandy when Duke William II conquered King Harold II of England at the Battle of Hastings in 1066 and became King William I of England, William the Conqueror. Since then, except for a few years, the island has been associated with the Crown of England.

At the time of the English Civil War, Prince Charles, later King Charles II, and Prince James, later King James II, found sanctuary in the island when they were excluded from all other parts of the King's dominions.

Queen Victoria and Prince Albert visited Jersey in 1846 and again in 1859, King George V, Queen Mary and the Princess Mary in 1921, and King George VI and Queen Elizabeth in 1945 following the Liberation. The present Queen visited the island with Prince Philip in 1949 before she succeeded to the throne, and as Sovereign in 1957 and 1989. Other members of the Royal Family, including Queen Elizabeth the Queen Mother, have visited Jersey from time to time.

Evidence of the royal connections abound in Jersey. There are statues to King George II, Queen Victoria and King George V. There are three royal societies connected with the island – the Royal Channel Islands Yacht Club, the Royal Jersey Agricultural and Horticultural Society and the Royal Jersey Golf Club – and over the years various tradesmen have been granted royal warrants of appointment. Victoria College is named after Queen Victoria and the Sovereign is Visitor of the College. In addition a number of buildings and thoroughfares are named after English Kings, Queens and other royal personages.

The cover of the Parish of St Helier Official Programme of celebrations to mark the Diamond Jubilee of Queen Victoria. (22 June 1897)

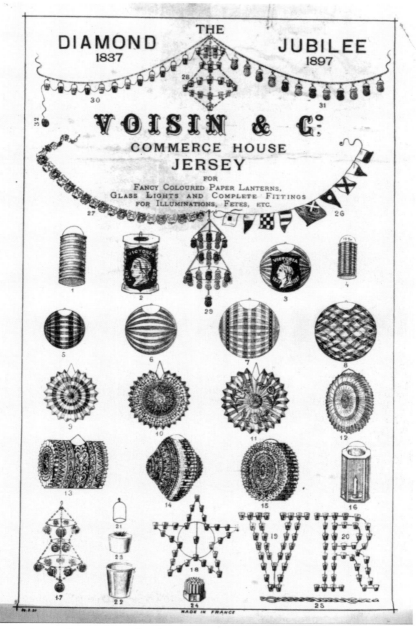

Voisin & Co.'s advertisement for decorations at the time of Queen Victoria's Diamond Jubilee. (1897)

Beresford Street, St Helier, decorated for the Diamond Jubilee. (1897)

Diamond Jubilee decorations at the Central Market, Halkett Place & Beresford Street, St Helier. (1897)

Broad Street, St Helier, at the time of the Diamond Jubilee. (1897)

Statue of Queen Victoria at the centre of the Weighbridge Gardens. The statue has been moved to the Victoria Park (formerly the Triangle Park), West Park, and the gardens have been removed. (1925)

Flags out for the Diamond Jubilee at Queen Street, St Helier. (1897)

Death of Queen Victoria, Weighbridge Gardens, St Helier. The Constable gave permission for the harbour master to open the gardens to the public to place their floral tributes around the Queen's statue. For another view of the same scene see *A Second Selection*, p. 141. (February 1901)

The Le Geyt Homes, St Saviour. These were 'erected in reverent loving memory of the great & good Queen 1837 R. Victoria 1901 by her dutiful & devoted servant & subject R.A. Le Geyt 1902'. (1908)

The Victoria Cottage Homes, St Saviour. These homes were built by the States of Jersey in 1902 to commemorate the Diamond Jubilee of Queen Victoria. (1905)

King George V, Queen Mary and HRH The Princess Mary at Springfield during their visit to Jersey. (1921)

Parishioners waiting at St John to see the royal party drive by during the afternoon of their visit to Jersey. (1921)

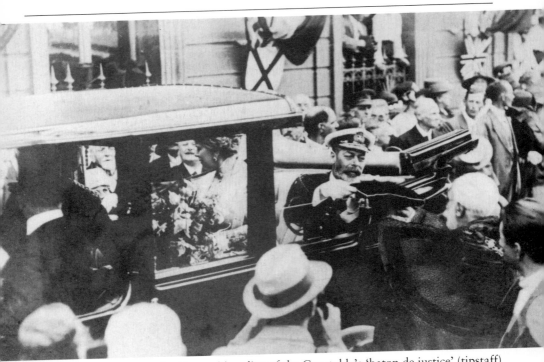

The King being presented with a gold replica of the Constable's 'baton de justice' (tipstaff) by the Constable of St Helier on behalf of the parishioners as a memento of his visit. (1921)

Victorian china dish bearing the inscription 'J. Pope Confectioner To Her Majesty 38, Halkett Place.' Whether the proprietor had any right to claim royal patronage is open to doubt as in those days the display of the royal arms and the claim of royal patronage were often made without authority.

The royal party at Springfield, St Helier. (1921)

His Excellency the Lieutenant-Governor Major General Sir J.M.R. Harrison, CB, DSO, in full dress uniform. (1939)

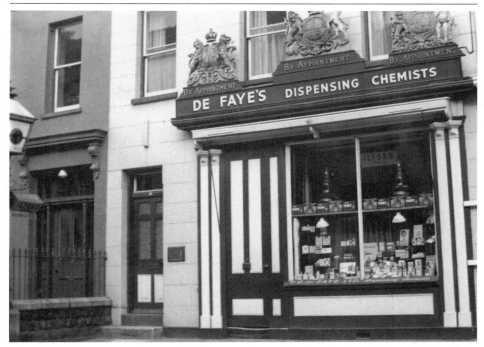

De Faye's, dispensing chemists, David Place, St Helier. The chemists displayed three coats of arms representing the three royal warrants of appointment granted to the proprietor by Queen Alexandra, Queen Mary and Princess Christian as manufacturer of eau-de-cologne. (1950s or '60s)

Levée at Government House, St Saviour. (8 June 1939)

Statue of King George V at the Howard Davis Park, St Helier, just after being unveiled by the Lieutenant-Governor Major General Sir J.M.R. Harrison. The sculptor was Sir William Reid Dick. (30 September 1939)

HRH The Duchess of Kent during her visit to Jersey to lay the foundation stone of the Nurses Home, Gloucester Street, St Helier. (June 1948)

TRH The Duke and Duchess of Gloucester arriving at the airport. (1952)

The Duchess of Gloucester, wearing a Jersey sun-bonnet, converses with Miss Godfray who is dressed in old Jersey costume and also wears a Jersey sun-bonnet. (1952)

The Proclamation of Accession being read by the Deputy Viscount on a platform in front of the statue of King George II in the Royal Square, St Helier. (6 February 1952)

A huge crown suspended above the road at the junction of Bath Street, Minden Place and Phillips Street, St Helier. This was one of the decorations put up in honour of the coronation of Queen Elizabeth II. (1953)

The British Hotel, Broad Street, St Helier, decorated in honour of the coronation of Queen Elizabeth II. The hotel was established in 1810. Although the exterior of the building remains unchanged, it is now occupied by a bank. (1953)

Queen Elizabeth II and the Duke of Edinburgh at Springfield, St Helier. (25 July 1957)

HRH The Princess Margaret, accompanied by His Excellency the Lieutenant-Governor General Sir George Erskine, GCB, KBE, DSO, entering the ballroom at West Park Pavilion (now the Inn on the Park), West Park, St Helier, for a Charity Ball. (25 June 1959)

HM Queen Elizabeth the Queen Mother, talking with the Very Reverend A.S. Giles, CB, CBE, MA, Dean of Jersey and Rector of St Helier, in the churchyard of the town church. (10 May 1963)

SECTION SEVEN

People and Events

The engines of the sunken vessel, the *Caledonia*, after being raised at low tide under the superintendence of Captain Nuttall. (July 1881)

Royal Militia Island of Jersey in camp on Mutton's Field, adjacent to Fort Regent, St Helier. (In or before 1906)

Church Parade, marching along La Motte Street after attending service at St James's, the Garrison church, St James's Street, St Helier. (In or before 1907)

A postcard issued to commemorate the Concours Musicale de Jersey. (1907)

St Clement's Show, Samarès Manor. (1907)

1st East Surrey Regiment on Grouville Common (Between 1905 and 1908)

The Garrison trooping the colour at Fort Regent, St Helier. (June 1909)

A family out for a drive. (Early this century)

Jersey Free Church Council's treat for five hundred poor children. (2 January 1914)

Jersey District Nursing Association. The Dean is pictured with some of the ladies who took a great interest in the work of the association. (February 1914)

Inspection of vehicles. The Constable of St Helier is inspecting vehicles for which the owners desired a renewal of licence. (March 1914)

German prisoner of war camp, Blanches Banques. (Between 1915 and 1919)

Rear of the funeral procession for Konrad Flechsig, a soldier in the 243rd Infantry Regiment of the German Army, who died at the prisoner of war camp at Blanches Banques on 12 May 1916, aged thirty-nine. (13 May 1916)

The glass hearse preceded by eight German soldiers carrying wreaths for the funeral of Konrad Flechsig. (13 May 1916)

The main body of mourners at Konrad Flechsig's funeral, with the rear of the band made up of sixteen German musicians from the POW camp. (13 May 1916)

Konrad Flechsig's funeral procession alongside the churchyard of St Brelade's church. The road is lined with men of the Hampshire Regiment with arms reversed. (13 May 1916)

Konrad Flechsig's funeral procession enters the churchyard. (13 May 1916)

Konrad Flechsig's coffin, covered with the German flag on which rested the deceased's service cap, borne on the shoulders of six soldiers from the 243rd Infantry Regiment. (13 May 1916)

Funeral of Konrad Flechsig. A side view of the band marching beside the church. (13 May 1916)

Pupils of the Jersey Ladies College (now the Jersey College for Girls). (*c.* 1916)

Royal Militia Island of Jersey marching along New Street, St Helier, on their way to take part in the 158th Anniversary Service of the Battle of Jersey at the town church. (January 1939)

Army Technical School, St Peter's Barracks, St Peter. This inspection was led by His Excellency the Lieutenant-Governor Major General Sir H. de C. Martelli, KBE, CB, DSO. (21 February 1939)

Exhibition of dancing arranged by Miss Jeanette Boielle, Springfield Theatre, St Helier. The dance being performed was called 'Memoirs de Louis XV'. (March 1939)

HMS *Jersey*, a 'J' Class destroyer launched on 26 September 1938, on her visit to Jersey. She was sunk on 2 May 1941 in the entrance to the Grand Harbour, Valetta, Malta. (1939)

German fortification astride the seawall bordering St Aubin's Bay in course of demolition. (1950s)

Breton musicians and folk-dancers, Mont Orgueil Castle, St Martin. (Probably 1952)

Breton Stilt Men proceeding eastwards along Queen Street, St Helier. The premises of both Messrs A. Amy & Son Ltd and Messrs G.D. Laurens have been demolished and rebuilt. (Probably 1952)